Wasp and Bee Management
A Common-Sense Approach

Written by

Jody Gangloff-Kaufmann

New York State IPM Program
Cornell University

NRAES–185
October 2011

ISBN 978-1-933395-22-7

Library of Congress Cataloging-in-Publication Data

Gangloff-Kaufmann, Jody Lynn
    Wasp and bee management : a common-sense approach / Jody
Gangloff-Kaufmann.
      p. cm. -- (NRAES ; 185)
    Includes bibliographical references.
    ISBN 978-1-933395-22-7
  1. Wasps. 2. Bees. 3. Wasps--Integrated control. 4. Bees--Integrated
control. I. Natural Resource, Agriculture, and Engineering Service.
Cooperative Extension. II. Title. III. Series: NRAES (Series) ; 185.
SB945.W3G36 2011
632'.79--dc23
                                                2011023501

Disclaimer

To order additional copies, contact:

Natural Resource, Agriculture, and Engineering Service (NRAES)
Cooperative Extension
PO Box 4557, Ithaca, New York 14852-4557
Phone: (607) 255-7654 • Fax: (607) 254-8770
Email: NRAES@CORNELL.EDU • Web site: WWW.NRAES.ORG

Cover photo: A female Carpenter bee, T. DeTerlizzi

Contents

(continued on next page)

Contents (cont.)

Acknowledgments

The author would like to thank the following peer reviewers for their invaluable input:

Sharon McCombs Apperson, apiarist; Lynn Braband, New York State IPM Program, Cornell University; Nicholas W. Calderone, Department of Entomology, Cornell University; Dewey M. Caron, University of Delaware Cooperative Extension; Whitney Cranshaw, Department of Bioagricultural Science and Pest Management, Colorado State University; James F. Dill, University of Maine Cooperative Extension; Christine Cairns Fortuin, USEPA, Atlanta, GA; Gary Fish, State of Maine Board of Pesticides Control; Daniel Gilrein, Cornell Cooperative Extension of Suffolk County; Craig Hollingsworth, Department of Plant, Soil, and Insect Sciences, University of Massachusetts; Steven B. Jacobs, Department of Entomology, Penn State University; David K. Jefferson, University of the District of Columbia; Carolyn Klass, Department of Entomology, Cornell University; Mary Kosenski, beekeeper, Tinton Falls, NJ; Peter J. Landolt, USDA–ARS, Wapato, WA; J. Peter Leighton, beekeeper, Jackson, NJ; Jeffrey D. Lunden, Department of Plant Pathology, Washington State University; Mary Kay Malinoski, Home and Garden Information Center, University of Maryland; W. Jay Nixon, American Pest Management, Inc., Takoma Park, MD; Jane Nogaki, New Jersey Environmental Federation, Marlton, NJ; Jay Paxson, University of Nevada Cooperative Extension; William Sciarappa, Rutgers Cooperative Extension; Margaret Siligato, University of Rhode Island; and Dennis vanEngelsdorp, Pennsylvania Department of Agriculture.

The book was edited by Holly Hyde and designed by Yen Chiang, NRAES. Aquillah White assisted with design. The project was managed by Marty Sailus.

About the Author

Jody Gangloff-Kaufmann is a Senior Extension Associate with the New York State Integrated Pest Management (IPM) Program at Cornell University and specializes in urban entomology and community IPM. She earned her Ph.D. from the Department of Entomology at Cornell University in the field of agricultural entomology. She was inspired to pursue her degree by Bernd Heinrich's book entitled *Bumblebee Economics*.

Preface

This book was written for a general audience including homeowners, buildings and grounds managers, Master Gardeners, landscapers, and pest-management professionals. The recommendations within are meant for application in a variety of settings where wasps and bees may be a nuisance or threat to people, especially in schools where the use of integrated pest management (IPM) is often required. IPM is a sustainable approach to controlling pests in ways that minimize negative human health and environmental impacts while also remaining economically feasible. There are many ways to discourage, deter, build out, and control wasps and bees, but the key is to understand when and where action is necessary. It is also important to use the best combination of tools for each situation. This book outlines many nonchemical control options that have been used for wasp and bee management. It does not provide insecticide recommendations because laws and pesticide availability vary by state.

It is very important to manage wasps and bees in a safe manner and to protect others from stings because allergic reactions to stings can be severe in some people. It is also necessary to respect the beneficial role these insects play in the environment. This book will help the reader determine whether and how best to manage wasps and bees in the human environment.

Chapter 1

Wasps and Bees

Considering the great diversity of wasps and bees in the Northeast, only a relatively small number pose risks to humans. One should always consider whether the wasps or bees encountered are problematic, and the tradeoffs of managing versus tolerating the insects. Chapter 2 of this guidebook gives the reader some basic tools for correctly identifying and understanding the species of wasp or bee in question. This chapter reviews wasp and bee management and stings.

Managing with IPM

When managing pests, always follow the principles of integrated pest management (IPM). IPM is a sustainable approach to controlling pests in ways that minimize negative human health and environmental impacts while also remaining economically feasible. IPM approaches include anticipation and prevention of pest problems and correct pest identification. It may also include cultural, biological, physical, and chemical means of control, using pesticides carefully and only when necessary.

An action threshold, or the point at which action is taken, is fundamental in many IPM programs. However, it can be challenging to determine an action threshold for wasps or bees because a single insect can pose serious health risks to an allergic person, yet wasps and bees are abundant outdoors. The Maryland Department of Agriculture suggests the following action thresholds for school IPM programs:

- Bees (honey) – Classrooms, kitchen, and public areas: 1 bee; maintenance areas: 3 bees; outdoors: no action unless children are threatened.

- Bees (bumble) – Classrooms, kitchen, and public areas: 1 bee; maintenance areas: 3 bees; outdoors: action necessary if communal nests are present in student activity area. Also, action whenever children are threatened.

- Bees (carpenter) – Classrooms, kitchen, and public areas: 1 bee; maintenance areas: 3 bees; outdoors: 1 carpenter bee/5 linear feet if susceptible, unfinished wood. Also, action whenever children are threatened.

- Yellow jackets/hornets – Classrooms and other public areas: 1 yellow jacket or hornet; outdoors: action necessary if nests are present in or near student activity area; 10/10 minutes at trash can or dumpster; 1 yellow jacket or hornet anywhere if children are threatened.

For many, the first management action, or reaction, is to spray an insecticide. However, the recommended long-term solution is prevention of wasp and bee problems by eliminating attractants, food sources, and shelter. There are ways to physically manage wasps and bees as alternative practices to using insecticides. If insecticides are necessary, only a product labeled for that pest should be used. All insecticides must be used in accordance with the label directions. The right formulation and active ingredient, plus the correct use of that product, can determine the success of the effort, therefore minimizing the amount of material needed. This guide does not cover pesticide recommendations because pesticide product registrations and laws vary from state to state. Consult with your state's lead agency on pesticides for more information.

An integrated pest management plan for wasps and bees includes the following:

❑ Correct identification of the insect
❑ Inspection, monitoring, and record keeping
❑ Management steps
  • Sanitation and food source reduction
  • Nest removal and exclusion
  • Trapping
  • Chemical controls (when necessary)
❑ Prevention of future problems

Inspection and Monitoring

Beginning in late May or early June, walk the perimeter of buildings and through playgrounds or landscapes to scout for wasp and bee activity, especially on warm, sunny days. Paper wasp nest initiation begins in May and peaks in July in the Northeast, but varies with temperature (warmer weather encourages insect growth and development). Paper wasps can be very active through late September, although new nests are not as common after late July. Yellow jacket colonies may go unnoticed until late July, but can be located with attentive early-season inspection. Check along the roofline of buildings using the sky as a backdrop. Look for wasps coming and going along eaves, in doorways, around windows, along the foundation, and in flower beds. Slowly lift boards on the ground and store them upright. Pay close attention to fence lines, especially wood picket or post-and-rail fences. Underground yellow jacket colonies are common in protected areas where grass grows higher or in cavities left by rotted posts or rodents. Yellow jackets also build colonies in stacked straw bales, and wood and compost piles.

Structures, such as fences, bleachers, furniture, playground equipment, bicycle racks, and other items in the landscape will also need to be scouted for wasp activity. Paper wasps will build small nests in metal fence pipes and hollow tubes of playground equipment, under bleachers and seats, and in any protected location. Plastic is not as attractive as wood and metal, but hollow plastic playground toys may become occupied. Paper wasp nests are sometimes visible in protected overhangs and under loose flashing, but may also be hidden inside cavities. By comparison, yellow jacket nests are usually built in sturdier, less open cavities with larger interior space.

Aerial yellow jackets usually build aboveground nests on the sides of buildings, inside storage sheds, and in

Figure 1.1   European paper wasps nesting in a pipe.

trees and shrubs, but can also build large colonies in small spaces. Some playground equipment is made of hollow logs and chains—be especially aware of wasp activity in these structures. In such a situation aerial yellow jackets will become very aggressive in response to the activity of children and pose a considerable risk to those nearby.

Bald-faced hornet nests, also built on structures, high up in trees, or in shrubs, may be concealed by foliage and not noticed until they are very large. These nests are easily spotted on structures, but one must pay close attention to vine-covered exterior walls, which provide excellent camouflage. Shrubs in areas of concern (such as school or park playgrounds) should be inspected in late June or July for wasp nests.

Figure 1.2 A bald-faced hornet nest in the landscape.

Established honey bee colonies in structures may be evident as early as late February or March, as warmer daytime temperatures allow limited foraging for early spring flowers. Preventive measures include inspecting the building and caulking small holes before a pest takes up residence. Highly susceptible areas include window and door frames, soffits, and anywhere that walls meet. Never seal a colony of bees, wasps, or other pests inside a structure as they will likely make their way inside the building.

Honey bee swarms are common throughout the spring and again during the late summer or early-fall nectar flows. Swarms are often observed as basketball-sized clusters of bees hanging on a branch, chimney, gutter, or other structure. Generally, swarms are not defensive, although they should be avoided. They will usually depart their landing site within one to three days. Local beekeepers are often willing to capture structure-infesting colonies and swarms. This process is intensive and takes time, but it preserves a potentially valuable colony.

Bumble bees are opportunistic and will occupy small structural cavities with openings close to the ground, as well as loose piles of organic matter, such as compost piles, hay bales, or thick thatch in hay fields. Bees coming and going may present a problem for nearby human activity. Make note of where these colonies exist, and if they pose a problem, keep people away until a management decision can be made.

Mud dauber and potter wasp activity will be evident in midsummer as females build mud tubes and pots on structures. These wasps often sun themselves on railings and decks, where they are commonly seen. Their nest-building activity should be noted if mud presents an aesthetic problem; however, the nests are fairly small and usually go unnoticed or can be tolerated.

Wasps and bees in the landscape, such as cicada killers, sand wasps, digger wasps, and ground-nesting bees, may only be noticed at the peak of their activity. It may

R. Blohm

Figure 1.3   Harvesting a honey bee swarm.

Figure 1.4   A mason wasp nest on a window frame.

be wise to cordon off an area where wasps or bees are active until a management decision can be made. Often these issues resolve in a short period of time because the window of activity is narrow for solitary wasps and bees. Habitat alteration can be useful (see "Nest Removal and Exclusion on page 12).

Record Keeping

All sound professional IPM programs require good record keeping. A wasp and bee management program will be most successful if details are recorded, such as nest locations, species present, actions taken, and pesticides applied. This will be especially important in institutional settings, such as schools, where pesticide use records must be kept. Wasps and bees will build nests in the same places each year if the sites are good. Nest location records should be used as a reference for repairs to the structure during winter months that will exclude wasps or bees when warm weather returns, and also to target future monitoring. Noting which species are present will aid in evaluating risk and deciding on control methods. By recording actions taken and pesticides used, one can evaluate whether methods are working and make appropriate changes. Record keeping also helps to justify actions taken.

Prevention, Sanitation, and Food Removal

Some yellow jackets are scavengers and will forage near food and garbage containers, particularly in the late summer through fall. Limiting the availability of food will directly reduce problems with wasps, as well as with other pests. Foraging preferences of social wasps change over the course of the season. Wasps search for protein in spring through late summer to provide food for developing larvae.

Once the colony peaks in late summer and wasps become most numerous, they are often noticed around sources of sugar, such as orchards with fallen fruit and outdoor activities where soda and juice are available. Covered garbage containers are recommended to reduce wasp foraging. To reduce attractiveness of trash containers, hose or power-wash them with soapy water each time they are emptied, or at least once a week. Replace broken and missing dumpster and trash can lids and keep them closed. Enclose waste in good-quality, sealed bags to prevent spills. Wash down milk crates after a delivery of milk or soda if they are left outside, since yellow jackets are attracted to residues from these liquids. Clean up any soda spills quickly and keep food and garbage covered inside the concession area. If fruit trees—including apple, crabapple, cherry, pear, or any other tree bearing sweet fruits—are present in the landscape, the fallen, overripe fruits should be picked up regularly to avoid creating a busy foraging ground for yellow jackets and paper wasps in early fall. If a seasonal problem exists, consider removing the fruit tree and replacing it with a shade tree.

Pet food, dead animals, compost piles, and other protein sources may become attractive to wasps as food, so it is important to make efforts to eliminate these attractants. Additionally, old wood structures, unpainted furniture, cardboard, wood chips, and dead trees or limbs are attractive to paper-nest-building wasps as they collect wood fiber for nest construction. If wasps are presenting a risk to people, remove dead limbs or paint the furniture and exposed wood to discourage wasps. The European hornet is known to girdle young trees, shrubs, or limbs as it peels bark to feed on sap. It may be necessary to create some kind of barrier if this behavior is common enough

J. Gangloff-Kaufmann

Figure 1.5   Wasps are attracted to food waste.

to cause damage to valuable trees and shrubs. The crushed bodies of nest mates are also attractive to wasps, due to the release of alarm pheromones. It is wise to avoid crushing yellow jackets or other large-colony wasps.

Figure 1.6   Paper wasp gathering wood fiber for nest-building.

Adult bees and solitary wasps typically feed on flower nectar and pollen and do not present a problem around food or garbage. White clover is a common weed in lawns, playgrounds, and athletic fields, and is usually tolerated. When white clover blooms, it provides a favorite food source for nectar-feeding wasps and bees, thereby posing some risk to anyone with bare feet. It may be necessary to manage clover in lawn areas used by children to avoid stings. Overseed the turfgrass aggressively, correct the pH (acidic soils favor clover growth), mow the clover blossoms regularly, and if absolutely necessary, use a selective herbicide as a spot spray to reduce clover.

To feed their young, some Scoliid wasps hunt in grassy

areas for May and June beetle grubs that feed on the roots of turfgrass, while digger wasps search for grasshoppers and crickets. For the short period of time that these wasps forage they can be numerous and cause athletic field managers to close fields out of caution. Although there is no risk of injury from digger wasps (they do not sting), management may be desired. Insecticides can be used to kill grubs, but an integrated strategy is recommended for long-term control. Controlling grasshoppers and crickets is not recommended. Further reading for the management of insects in turfgrass can be found in the Additional Resources section of this guidebook (page 86).

Nest Removal and Exclusion

Remember: Individuals sensitive or allergic to stings should not conduct this work. If they must be involved, however, sensitive people should wear protective clothing, such as a bee suit, and carry an epinephrine shot prescribed by their physician when doing any wasp or bee colony removal. Any person who is inexperienced working with wasps and bees should not work from a ladder due to the risk of falling and injury if wasps or bees become alarmed. If the colony is out of reach but still a threat, call a professional pest manager.

Using a pole, a hose with a powerful nozzle, or a power-washer, remove visible paper-wasp nests from eaves and structures every two weeks from early June through July. Be sure to destroy the nest and kill workers that have dropped to the ground. Studies show this approach is effective in reducing paper-wasp nests for the whole summer. Painted or varnished surfaces may discourage paper-wasp nesting. A practice common in tropical regions is to paint the underside of wood porches, stairs, and railings a sky blue color to deter nest building. After several tests, minimal evidence was found to confirm this as effective. It could be that simply painting the underside of a porch in any color discourages nest building.

Locating a yellow jacket nest within a wall cavity can be difficult. Often professional pest managers use stethoscopes to listen for gnawing and buzzing. Some professionals have adopted the use of thermal-imaging cameras to locate wasp and bee colonies within walls, as well as other pest activity. A yellow jacket nest in a structural cavity is difficult to remove without tearing down walls. However, the strength and size of the colony can be quickly reduced by vacuuming workers as they come and go. Once a structural cavity nest is identified, all possible entrances should be located and blocked, except for one main outdoor entryway. Make every effort to find openings that lead into the occupied part of the structure-

Figure 1.7   Vacuuming a yellow jacket nest entrance.

such as living spaces, offices, or classrooms-and seal them up. Canister-style vacuums are more easily maneuvered, and the hose is generally longer and can be easily sealed with tape or a rag. Wasps should be collected into a new vacuum bag. A cloth HEPA-type bag is stronger than a paper bag, but either type will work. An alternative to collecting wasps inside a vacuum, which can present a problem of what to do next, is to collect them into a device as described in the accompanying sidebar.

Yellow Jacket Vacuum Trap

Designed by Fred Ludewig, Master Gardener, Cornell Cooperative Extension, Saratoga County, NY

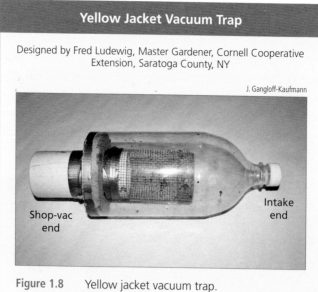

J. Gangloff-Kaufmann

Shop-vac end

Intake end

Figure 1.8   Yellow jacket vacuum trap.

Materials List:

- 2-liter soda bottle with the bottom removed
- Wood ring, 2⅜ inch inside diameter, 4¼ inch outside diameter, ⅜ inch thick
- 2-inch diameter PVC pipe, 5 inches long
- Wood plug 2⅜ inch diameter, ¾ inch thick

continued on next page...

With either method, make sure the vacuum has a clean filter. Always wear protective clothing, such as gloves, head protection (a bee veil) and even a bee suit or other light-colored protective clothing. Begin vacuuming in the morning as wasp activity starts to increase. Hold or secure the vacuum hose end within two inches of the open entrance for an hour or as long as it takes to reduce the frequency of activity. The wasps coming and going through the entrance will be collected into the vacuum. It is possible to collect thousands of wasps in one hour, dur-

...continued from p.14
- 8 mesh screen, 4 inches by 8½ inches
- Staple gun, duct tape, shop-vac vacuum

Assembly:
- Attach rolled-up screen around the wood plug with staples
- Attach the other end of rolled-up screen to PVC pipe with duct tape
- Slide wood ring over PVC pipe
- Slide soda bottle over wood ring and attach with staples, seal with duct tape.

Operating:
Remove soda bottle cap. Connect PVC pipe to the shop-vacuum hose. Place open end of soda bottle close to yellow jacket colony entrance and let run for two hours (or so). Replace soda bottle cap. Remove bottle from shop-vacuum hose and place device into the freezer to kill yellow jackets. The vacuuming procedure may need to be repeated in 2 weeks as new yellow jackets hatch. For those who routinely manage yellow jackets, this tool is recommended because it offers the advantage of separating captured wasps from the vacuum.

ing peak traffic times. Wasps should not become alarmed if the vacuum is vented away from the colony, but they are often wary of the hose, and some will learn to avoid it. Repositioning or actively directing the hose may be necessary. Once vacuuming is finished, the end of the hose should be sealed with tape and the vacuum placed in a black plastic bag in the sun for the duration on one day. Alternatively, use suction to collect a small amount of sand to stun the wasps, and then seal the hose end. Leave the vacuum in a safe location outdoors for two days, and most or all wasps will be killed. This can be repeated once a week to reduce wasp activity, or combined with the subsequent application of an approved insecticidal dust to the nest cavity entrance (as far in as can be reached) for a quick kill. Vacuuming at least once will minimize the number of dead insects inside the void when following up with an insecticide.

Exclusion of wasps from equipment and fences should be done early in the spring. Use hardening/expanding foam to fill small cavities where nest building occurs. If an active nesting site is sealed up during summer, it should be done at night. It may be necessary to temporarily cordon off the area from people to avoid contact with alarmed wasps that have no access to their colony. In this case, another technique to kill remaining wasps may be needed. Keep in mind that wasps readily gnaw wood and will carve their way through foam or silicone caulk if they are trapped inside or determined to regain access to a void. Combining foam or caulk with steel or copper wool may reduce this problem, though permanent fixes are always better. Ideally exclusion should be done before nest building even begins, and a best practice is to use scouting reports from the previous year to identify problematic

Figure 1.9   Sealing a wall void to exclude yellow jackets.

openings that should be sealed up during cold weather.

Do not attempt to seal up active structural nests in occupied buildings from the outside, even if an insecticide was used, because adult wasps will then be forced inside the structure and can present a serious hazard to building occupants. Structural cavities should only be sealed during the winter months to ensure that no live wasps are trapped inside. When sealing entryways, it is preferable to make permanent repairs that exclude pests, such as filling access points with concrete and replacing damaged wood. However, this is not always feasible, so the use of temporary fixes, such as sealing cavities with copper wool and insulation foam, are recommended. Metal flashing on buildings must be pinned down and secured to eliminate spaces for paper wasps to nest. Weep holes can be covered or blocked with copper wool or other barriers that eliminate pest access. See Additional Resources (page 86) for more information.

Honey bees that have taken up residence within a structure can pose a serious problem. If treated with pesticides, the colony will die, and the remaining brood and honey will attract pests like mice, dermestid beetles, wax moths, filth flies, ants, and other insects. The leftover honey will ferment, causing unpleasant odors, and honey may seep through walls and ceilings creating further damage. Never kill a honey bee colony in a valued structure without also removing the remains of the colony. Unfortunately, proper abatement can be an involved process, often requiring removal of sections of ceilings, walls, floors and siding to access the bees and nest. Once exposed, removal of the bees and nest can be accomplished with a shop-vacuum, scraping tools, buckets, and heavy-duty garbage bags to hold the comb and debris. An approved insecticide can be used to kill the bees if necessary; however, insecticide-treated honey must be removed and disposed of, never consumed. Yellow jackets that have been killed in their nests with insecticides should also be removed. Although

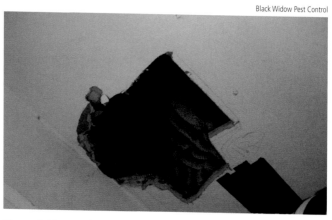

Figure 1.10   Ceiling cut open to remove a honey bee colony.

yellow jackets do not store honey, leftover brood can attract mice and dermestid beetles. It may be necessary to hire a contractor to repair the ceilings or walls.

Deterrents can be used for cicada killer wasps and ground-nesting bees. The daily overhead irrigation of nesting areas over a period of time can be an effective deterrent. Irrigation must be provided for an extended period of time to saturate the ground, and during the day while wasps and bees are active. Tarps placed for a few days over the area used for nesting will also discourage nesting in the area. Long-term deterrents for cicada killer wasps and ground-nesting bees involve habitat modification. Thick turfgrass, appropriate ground-cover plants, and mulch make a site unattractive for burrowing. Removal or thinning of trees can reduce the number of female cicada killer wasps in a nearby field by lowering cicada activity. In playgrounds, the use of wood, rubber mulch, or pebbles can reduce site attractiveness for wasps and bees. If sand is preferred as a substrate, such as under playground equipment, remove the top four inches of sand, install weed-barrier fabric, and replace the sand, to create an obstruction to ground-nesting wasps and bees. This will also reduce weed problems.

Trapping

Although pheromones have been shown to attract wasps in specific cases, pheromone attractants are not available for use on wasps or bees. Trapping, using food-based attractants, has value in specific situations. In particular, when a yellow jacket nest cannot be located or if a colony of yellow jackets exists on neighboring private property (and cannot be treated), traps can temporarily reduce the number of foraging wasps in the area of concern. In addition, traps are useful for reducing wasp numbers before events or gatherings. For trapping to be most effective, alternative food sources must be minimized. Thorough cleaning of food service areas and waste handling that reduces wasp attraction (for example, placing trash away from the gathering area) are essential for a trapping program to be successful.

Traps should be set at a height of about six feet and along the perimeter of an area to be protected, and they should be placed more than ten feet away from food service and eating areas. Trapping in preparation for a gathering should be done during the week before the event and can be continued during the event. Although studies show that totally wasp-free zones are not usually created using traps, using baited wasp traps ahead of time alleviates the nuisance these wasps create around people.

Some traps that can be purchased are baited with volatile chemical attractants and collect wasps into a dry cone. Since attractants lose effectiveness over time, traps should be replenished according to manufacturer recommendations. Other traps will collect wasps into a liquid-filled catch basin. These traps must be cleaned and refreshed at least every two to three days. Recommended liquid baits are fruit punch; orange soda; pineapple, apple or pear juice; and beer. Try different baits to see which one attracts wasps at that particular site.

Several types of traps are available commercially. Traps shaped like a jar with openings at the top for wasp entry usually come with a tube of attractive liquid (nontoxic) bait. To improve the effectiveness of a jar-type trap, smear a one-inch-wide ring of petroleum jelly around the rim to prevent wasps from climbing out of the jar.

To make a homemade trap out of a two-liter soda bottle, cut off the top funnel, invert it, and tape it back into the bottle, making a down-facing funnel opening. Cut three pen-sized holes in the lower sides a few inches above the bottom, and fill the trap with liquid bait up to the holes. Set traps in sunny areas of wasp activity. Traps may be hung up or placed near garbage areas or on rooftops near playgrounds and other inconspicuous places, but must also be cleaned or disposed of every two to three days to avoid decay.

L. Braband

Figure 1.11   Traps positioned to reduce yellow jacket activity at the concession stand.

Insecticides for the Control of Wasps and Bees

After all these management tactics have been considered and/or used, and wasps or bees are still a problem, a pesticide may be needed. Insecticides vary in efficacy, toxicity, and in their risks to human health and the environment. Where possible, the lowest-impact products should be chosen first. Whether traditional or reduced-risk formulations are chosen, insecticides must be used with caution and according to label directions. In addition to label requirements, personal protective gear such as a bee veil or bee suit should be worn when using an insecticide spray or dust on a colony of wasps or bees. Applying pesticides on a cool night helps ensure that most workers are in the colony, and a more thorough job can be done. However, cool nights cannot be relied upon for reduced risk because wasps and bees will defend their nests in cool weather and in darkness. If a flashlight is to be used, cover the lens with red cellophane or tint with a red marker to reduce the visibility of light. Aggravated wasps will follow a light beam to its source if disturbed at night. Use protective clothing and work in pairs, one holding the flashlight and the other treating the nest. Spray around and into the entrance of the nest. Beware that pyrethrins and pyrethroids are irritating to wasps and can cause aggressive swarming. Several plant oil (botanical) products are repellant and can cause a colony to become agitated as well. Treat the nest, and quickly move away.

Both chemical and botanical insecticides are also formulated as long-distance sprays (15 – 20-foot reach), and working farther away from the nest can reduce risk to the applicator. Treat paper-wasp nests at night to ensure most members are on the comb. Do not stand under the colony when treating it. As workers fall to the ground, it may be necessary to crush them quickly before they fly off or toward you. Knock the nest down to prevent new queens from reoccupying it, and crush or dispose of the comb to prevent pupae from emerging.

When treating a wall void nest in a structure also occupied by people, first check that wasps have no entrance from the void into the building—into drop ceilings, vents, ducts, or rooms where people are living or working. If this can be confirmed (there are no dead wasps on windowsills or inside drop ceilings or light fixtures), vacate the room or home, and treat the colony in the evening when wasps have returned to the colony. Dusts work best for cavities. If it is possible that wasps have access to the inside of the building, treat from the inside out, or treat from the outside when the building will be unoccupied for two or three days. Do a follow-up visit to check the rooms, windows, and drop ceilings for live wasps before the occupants return. Removal of old nest materials is suggested but not always possible. Secondary pest problems generated by the remains of a colony can be reduced using desiccant dusts applied into the wall void.

When dealing with an aerial yellow jacket or bald-faced hornet colony, one may choose to treat the nest at night with a pyrethrin aerosol and wait a couple of days for activity to cease. While wearing protective gear, direct the spray into the nest entrance. Spray a light coating on the outside of the nest as well. Wasps will likely swarm for a period of time, so the area should be cordoned off from people and pets. An aerosol insecticide can be used for personal protection. When activity ceases, remove the nest, place it into a plastic garbage bag, and discard it. With any pesticide product, the applicator is required to read the label and follow label directions, as well as all state laws concerning the licensing of pesticide applicators. Many states require a license to apply pesticides as a part of a paid position or job.

Things you should NEVER do to control wasps and bees:

- Never pour gasoline into a ground or structural nest to kill wasps or bees. It is dangerous, illegal, and causes environmental damage.

- Never attempt to burn the nest—it is dangerous, ineffective, and will alarm the wasps or bees. Fires can also get out of control easily.

- Never block the entrance to a yellow jacket nest, especially if the entrance hole is on a building. Trapped yellow jackets can find or create an entry into the building interior endangering those inside. Filling in the hole of a ground nest during the day will cause alarmed yellow jackets to swarm.

- Never pour liquid insecticides into an individual ground-nesting wasp or bee burrow. This is an illegal application of the pesticide and ineffective in controlling solitary wasps and bees. Some dust formulations are labeled for application in burrows, if necessary.

- Never rely upon outdoor fogging or general (broadcast) spraying to control wasps or bees in a yard or public space. Broadcast insecticides are ineffective because wasps and bees are good fliers and travel great distances to forage. Also, more beneficials than pests will likely be killed.

IPM Checklist for Wasp and Bee Management (for Buildings and Grounds)

Late fall through early spring

❑ Recall any wasp and bee activity on or around the building, and eliminate access to nesting sites by sealing openings, repairing flashing, replacing missing bricks, filling rodent burrows, eliminating clutter such as wooden boards, and taking any other prevention steps as needed.

Early to late spring

❑ Monitor buildings and grounds for wasp and bee activity on a weekly basis, on sunny warm days.

Late spring through summer

❑ Destroy paper-wasp nests on buildings and in areas close to people using a strong jet of water, a long pole, or a low-risk pesticide product.

❑ Look for yellow jacket activity, including both colonies on site and foraging workers from colonies off site.

Late summer through fall

❑ Monitor buildings and grounds for wasp and bee activity on a weekly basis, on sunny warm days, and take action as necessary.

❑ If needed, use traps baited with orange soda or fruit punch to capture wasps in sensitive areas (playgrounds, for example).

❑ If yellow jacket activity is high, do a thorough search for a colony on site.

❑ Reduce attractiveness of the area using sanitation and other techniques described in the guidebook.

❑ Destroy yellow jacket colonies on site, using safe, effective techniques.

❑ Note where wasp and bee activity occurred through the year, and keep records if possible.

Winter

❑ Plan a prevention strategy for the following year.

❑ Raise awareness among building occupants and staff about pests and IPM.

❑ Permanently seal openings where yellow jackets, honey bees, or bumble bees have previously gained access.

❑ Fix flashing, and eliminate other sheltered spaces where paper wasps build nests.

Figure 1.12   Aerial yellow jackets guarding the nest entrance.

Wasp and Bee Stings

Encounters between humans and wasps and bees are inevitable, particularly since the more dangerous insect species are adapted to living on, in, and around human habitation. The major threats to humans are the risk of being stung by a wasp or bee and the toxic effects of the venom. The likelihood of a person being stung varies by insect species, but the consequences may not. Most people have been stung at least once in their lifetime; for most, the reaction is unpleasant with pain and swelling, but not life threatening. However, venom can injure or kill a person in two ways—by direct toxic effect of the venom involving a great number of stings, and by allergic reaction of some individuals to the venom. The allergic reaction of sensitive people is of most concern because the sting of just one insect can kill them. Many people are unaware of their sensitivity to stings.

First Response for Wasp and Bee Stings

A Single Sting

Lacking prominent barbs, wasps and most bees can quickly sting and fly away. Honey bees' stings are different. The honey bee worker has a barbed stinger and can only sting once. After stinging, the worker pulls away, ripping the stinger and venom sac from her body, resulting in its death. If not removed immediately, the venom sac continues to pump venom into the victim's tissues, and increased venom can enhance the reaction. Quick removal of the barbed stinger, within 15 seconds, is very important. Use a credit card or other flat item to scrape the stinger from the skin, or grip and pull it out. Research shows that, regardless of the method used to remove a stinger, the quicker it is removed, the less intense the reaction will be.

L. Braband

Figure 1.13   The second stinging insect-related death in the United States.

Once stung, the body's response is characterized by an increase in fluids at the sting site, which helps flush away the venom. Acute pain and lingering sensitivity at the sting site may happen as well. In nonallergenic people (those who do not suffer acute allergic reaction), a cold compress and antihistamine oral and topical treatments can reduce discomfort. If the person has been stung in the recent past, the localized reaction may be more severe, including such reactions as swelling of the entire limb and itching. Furthermore, a systemic reaction can occur that produces allergy symptoms in areas other than the sting site. This can be mild or in many cases severe, especially if the victim is stung again.

A small number of people (approximately two out of every 1,000) are highly allergic to wasp and bee venom and will suffer from a severe, systemic, possibly even life-threatening reaction to stings. If a person is suspected of developing a generalized allergic reaction (symptoms include weakness, difficulty breathing, generalized swelling, hives, abdominal cramps, vomiting, diarrhea, rapid pulse, and low blood pressure), IMMEDIATE medical attention is needed. Anaphylactic shock and even death could occur within 15 – 30 minutes in the worst case. If an individual is highly allergic to wasp or bee venom, that person should carry an epinephrine treatment prescribed by their own physician at all times and consider not working with wasps and bees.

Multiple Stings

Wasps and many bees have very small barbs on their stingers and can sting repeatedly. Alarmed wasps will produce pheromones that incite nest mates to act in defense;

therefore a victim may suffer multiple stings. When numerous stings occur, as can be expected when a person accidentally disturbs a colony of yellow jackets for example, mass envenomization may result. The risk of serious illness is much greater than if the victim is stung only once or twice. Multiple stings can cause generalized pain and sick feelings, but can be deadly if enough venom is injected. Although estimates vary, a healthy 165 lb (75 kg) adult would likely need to be stung between 800 and 1,500 times to be at risk of death. Clearly the lethal dose is lower for children and the elderly. In addition, a person who suffers multiple stings may be at risk of kidney problems. Venom breaks down proteins in the body, and this reaction can overburden the kidneys. Patients must be observed for several days after a multiple-sting incident.

Steps to Follow if a Person Is Stung:

- Get the person to a safe area to avoid more stings.

- Stay with the person to monitor for an allergic reaction.

- Remove the stinger, if necessary, by scraping or pulling it out as soon as possible.

- Use a cold compress on the sting site.

- Administer topical or oral antihistamines as needed for nonallergenic reactions.

- Apply a baking soda paste, made of 3 teaspoons of baking soda and 1 teaspoon of water to the site. This will draw out some of the venom.

- To avoid infection do not allow the victim to scratch the site of the sting.

- If signs of a severe reaction begin to appear, immediately call for emergency medical assistance! Call 911 or your local emergency service.

- While waiting for emergency help, have the victim lie down on his or her back with feet elevated.

- Loosen clothing, and cover the person with a blanket if available.

- If the victim is vomiting or bleeding from the mouth, turn him or her on their side to prevent choking.

- If the victim is not breathing and there are no signs of circulation, begin CPR immediately.

Prevention of Wasp and Bee Stings

The best prevention of stings begins with awareness of wasps and bees, their behavior, and their habitats. Simple precautions can be taken to reduce the risk of being stung:

- Perfumes and strong-smelling soaps and shampoos may attract wasps and bees. Avoid using fragrant products if you plan to be outdoors.

- Dark-colored or brightly patterned clothing is attractive, so wear light-colored clothes, especially when doing colony removal.

- Do not swat at a yellow jacket, or it may become alarmed and more aggressive. If a yellow jacket is crushed, the scent may attract nest mates to that area.

- Avoid walking barefoot in lawns with clover and other weed flowers, where the risk of stepping on a wasp or bee is high. Make sure children wear shoes or sandals when playing outside.

- Reduce clover in yards used frequently by people. Try overseeding with high-quality turfgrass seed to crowd out the clover. Use a lawn mower to cut away clover flowers a day in advance of using the area (for a summer party, for example). An application of a broadleaf herbicide may be justified to reduce flowering weeds and the risk of people being stung.

- If a wasp or bee lands on you, do not flick it off. Gently brush or blow it off.

- Scoop out wasps and bees caught in the swimming pool. If alive, they may sting.

- Be aware of ground and aerial yellow jacket nests developing in areas used by people. Early detection leads to the most successful and safe control.

- Insect repellent will not deter wasps and bees.

Chapter 2

Common Wasps and Bees of the Northeastern United States

Wasps and bees are part of a large group of insects, called the Order Hymenoptera, which represents some of the most highly advanced insects on earth, including ants. Wasps and bees are fascinating and complex in their structure, behavior, and ecological roles. They are considered among the most beneficial groups of insects from the human perspective, serving as pollinators of one-third of

J. Gangloff-Kaufmann

Figure 2.1   A bumble bee collecting nectar and pollinating.

Figure 2.2   Bald-faced hornet collecting wood fiber for nest construction.

food crops (responsible for nearly $15 billion yearly in US agriculture), as well as parasites and predators of pest insects.

Similarities among the wasps, bees, and ants include the development in many species of the truly social (eusocial) organization of a colony, which is defined by cooperation and a division of labor among nest mates. Sex, or gender, is usually determined by fertilization of the egg. Unfertilized eggs become male, fertilized eggs become female. In many species the egg-laying structure, or ovipositor, has been modified into a stinging organ with a venom sac for defense. Since this is a female organ, males of all species are unable to sting. There are often extreme modifications of the ovipositor into specialized egg-laying organs. Superficially, the wings of wasps, bees, and ants look similar. The forewing is greater in size than the hind wing, and they join together to form what appears as a single wing. Ants are numerous, complex, and pests of a different sort. They are not covered in this guide.

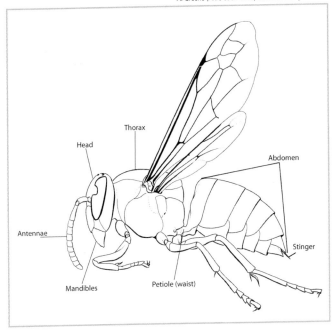

Figure 2.3   Basic anatomy of a wasp.

Only a few common species of wasps and bees pose significant risks to humans, such as injury from stings and damage to structures. These species tend to inhabit areas close to humans, such as man-made landscapes, buildings, objects, and other areas of human activity. Attracted by good colony building sites and food sources, some social wasps and bees can develop large colonies and will vigorously defend their resources when disturbed. Even solitary wasps and bees can pose real or perceived threats to humans. While not likely to sting for defense, solitary wasps and bees are often territorial and protective or inquisitive, and this behavior may be confused with aggression. Normally docile species may sting when handled or stepped on. Caution and healthy respect for wasps and bees is always advised.

Understanding the differences among commonly encountered wasps and bees will help in their management, when management is needed. This chapter covers some basic biology and ecology of major species found in the northeastern United States and describes best management practices, focusing on the use of nonchemical and integrated methods. It is organized by relative risk of human encounters with various species, from high risk to low, based on the threat of being stung, as well as suffering property damage.

Wasps and Bees Are Beneficial Insects

Wasps and bees are diverse in their biology and ecology. The positive aspects of wasps and bees must be taken into consideration as control decisions are made. Bees are important pollinators of fruit, flowers, and vegetables—without them, the food we love would be scarce.

Nearly all wasps are predators, many feeding upon pest insects. Yellow jackets, paper wasps, hornets, and many solitary wasps are predators of soft-bodied caterpillars that damage desirable plants in our gardens and landscapes.

Yellow jackets and paper wasps can have a positive impact on pests in agricultural fields and landscapes, possibly reducing the need for pesticides. The cicada killer wasp, an occasional nuisance in the landscape, helps protect trees by harvesting cicadas that feed on the roots and growing tips of branches. Management decisions for wasps and bees must be made with careful consideration. Control strategies should only be undertaken when a

Figure 2.4   Bumble bee on a coneflower.

Figure 2.5   Predatory mud dauber wasp with a caterpillar.

true threat exists or the nuisance these insects cause is intolerable. In addition, the conservation of beneficial bees and wasps should always be a goal. Visit the Xerces Society for Invertebrate Conservation for more information (www.xerces.org).

Paper-Nest-Building Social Wasps (High Risk)

Social wasps of the family Vespidae include the yellow jackets (*Vespula* and *Dolichovespula* species), hornets (*Vespa crabro*), and paper wasps (*Polistes* species). All groups are known for constructing papery nest structures, called cartons, from chewed cellulose material collected from sources such as fallen trees and wooden objects. Damage to cedar- or wood-sided homes has been reported as yellow jacket workers scrape wood to build nests. All nests are constructed in the form of combs with hexagonal or six-sided cells; some are single-layered and exposed, while others are built in tiers and wrapped in a paper envelope.

Most combs are constructed in protected areas, such as hollow walls in buildings, cavities inside or under stumps, and in trees and shrubs. Several species of yellow jackets will build colonies underground, often using abandoned rodent burrows. As colonies grow, they become a prized

G. Alpert

Figure 2.6   A single-layered paper comb.

Figure 2.7 Constructing the paper envelope for the comb.

food source for mammals, such as skunks and bears. As a result, social wasps will vigorously defend the colony by swarming and stinging. Because the stinger has very small barbs, wasps can sting repeatedly. Therefore, when in close proximity to humans or man-made structures, colonies must often be managed to protect people. Colonies located away from human activity or high in trees generally should not be of concern because they pose less risk.

Yellow Jackets

Large-Colony Scavenger/Predator Yellow Jackets; Small-Colony Non-Scavenger Yellow Jackets; Aerial-Nesting Yellow Jackets

At least thirteen species of yellow jackets are found in the northeastern United States. Several are notorious cavity- and ground-nesting species that will swarm when disturbed. Yellow jacket colonies can become quite large by late summer, and may contain thousands of workers in tiered layers of comb.

J. Gangloff-Kaufmann

Figure 2.8   Tiered layers of a yellow jacket nest with the envelope removed.

Colonies are easily overlooked early in the season when they are small but may become prominent in late summer because of the peak in worker numbers and the increase in activity that occurs during that time.

Colonies are started in spring by a single, mated

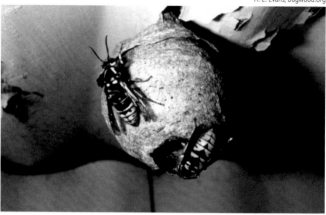

Figure 2.9   Queen and worker aerial yellow jackets building a paper nest.

queen. Queens are the only members of a colony to survive a northern United States winter, spending the season in dormancy in a protected spot. In the southern United States, queens and sometimes workers will survive colder months. Only about one percent of yellow jacket queens are successful in initiating a colony. Queens begin the colony by gathering wood pulp to create the first cells of the nest. The queen builds just enough cells in a comb to begin raising the first brood. She will be the sole provider for the first brood until they emerge as adult workers. The newly emerged wasps then take over the tasks of nest expansion, brood care, and foraging. The queen spends the rest of her life laying eggs. Colonies continue to grow through the summer.

During the time when the brood is being raised (spring through early fall), protein must be provided to developing larvae. Yellow jackets prey mainly upon other insects. They prefer large, soft-bodied insects like caterpil-

Figure 2.10   Eggs and larval wasps in a new nest.

Figure 2.11   A yellow jacket foraging in late summer.

lars; however, some species will also scavenge for animal carcasses, pet food, or food waste. Workers consume nectar or the juices of fruits for energy. In the fall, once a brood of future queens and males has matured and abandoned the colony to mate, the queen dies. Workers may linger through fall months and continue to forage for sugars. During this time, after the colony peaks, aggressive behavior increases while the colony's social structure collapses. Late summer into early fall is the time when yellow jackets commonly become troublesome in the human environment.

Several species of yellow jackets are commonly encountered in the northeastern United States, and these can be divided into three general categories based on their biology and ecology. The first includes the large-colony yellow jackets that are scavengers/predators and most often become pests of humans. These yellow jackets forage on garbage, carcasses, and human and animal food that has been left outdoors. The second category includes several less problematic species that have smaller colonies. They are not scavengers, but they can be found in human environments. These wasps prey only on live insects and are less likely to become serious pests (but they will sting). Both of these groups build nests in above- and belowground cavities. The third group consists of aerial-nesting yellow jackets, which are not typically scavengers. Colonies are normally constructed outside of structures, in trees and shrubs, and on the sides of structures. The aerial-nesting yellow jackets have smaller colonies, but are quite aggressive when disturbed.

German Yellow Jacket
Vespula germanica
Large-Colony Scavenger/Predator Yellow Jacket

J. Gangloff-Kaufmann

Figure 2.12 German yellow-jacket worker.

Worker Size
½ – ⅝ inch (14 – 16 mm)

Colony size
Up to 5,000+ workers

Colony locations
Natural or man-made cavity nests, subterranean

The German yellow jacket is an introduced species to North America and other parts of the world. It originated in Europe and is found throughout the northeastern United States. It is among the most commonly encountered pest yellow jackets in the Northeast. These wasps are scavengers as well as predators and often pose a threat to humans. Colonies are typically located in wall voids, attics, and other structures, and man-made items, but they will also nest underground and are sometimes found in cavities under discarded boards, stumps, or in rodent burrows. German yellow jackets build large nests of 3,500 to 15,000 cells in layered tiers, enclosed in a gray paper carton with scalloped edges. Even when nesting in a void, the colony will be at least partially enclosed in an envelope. The German yellow jacket is aggressive and is often accidentally encountered by people using lawnmowers near ground nests. This species will travel up to 1,300 yards (1,200 meters or ¾ mile) to forage for food. German yellow jacket workers may linger through November with warm weather.

Eastern Yellow Jacket
Vespula maculifrons
Large-Colony Scavenger/Predator Yellow Jacket

S.B. Jacobs

Figure 2.13 Eastern yellow jacket worker.

Worker Size
½ inch (14 mm)

Colony size
Up to 2,000 – 3,000 workers in the northeastern US, greater in the South

Colony locations
Subterranean, wood piles, compost bins, and various other cavities

The geographic range of the native eastern yellow jacket covers the entire eastern half of the United States to the Rocky Mountains. Colony size and duration are greater in the southern climate. In the Northeast, colonies are initiated in May or June and peak in late August or early September. Although the eastern yellow jacket is a primary pest in the Northeast, there is evidence that the German yellow jacket may be replacing it as the most important pest species. Both wasps occupy similar types of nesting cavities. Colonies are typically found below ground in yards, hardwood forests, creek banks, roadsides, rotting stumps, walls, leaf and compost piles, and other natural and man-made cavities. The comb is wrapped in a fragile tan-brown paper envelope. The eastern yellow jacket is a predator and scavenger for protein for developing larvae, but adults will also consume nectar and fruit juices.

Common Yellow Jacket
Vespula vulgaris
Large-Colony Scavenger/Predator Yellow Jacket

©2008 Gary McDonald

Figure 2.14 Common yellow jacket.

Worker Size
⅝ – ⅔ inch (17 – 20 mm)

Colony size
1,000 – 4,000 workers

Colony locations
Mainly subterranean and under logs or wood; occasionally in structural cavities and voids

The common yellow jacket is found throughout the northern hemisphere in the temperate and subarctic climates. It is a both a scavenger and a predator. Common yellow jacket queens tend to start colonies in natural cavities such as hollow trees, under logs, in ground cavities, and under tree stumps. Colonies may also occupy abandoned rodent burrows, and as the colony grows, soil is excavated to accommodate increasing nest size. The comb, although typically built in a protected location, is always partly enclosed in a paper envelope. As with most yellow jackets, workers collect insects to feed to developing larvae, but they may also collect protein from carcasses, garbage, and pet or human food. Adults will consume nectar and juices from fruit. Colonies of the common yellow jacket peak and decline in September and rarely appear as late as November.

Downy Yellow Jacket
Vespula flavopilosa
Large-Colony Scavenger/Predator Yellow Jacket

© 2008 Rich Kelly

Worker Size
½ inch (14 mm)

Colony size
Approximately 500 – 1,000 workers. Colony duration is shorter than other similar species.

Colony locations
Subterranean, as well as in structural voids

Figure 2.15   Downy yellow jacket.

The downy yellow jacket is quite similar to the eastern and common yellow jackets, both in markings and behavior. It is a scavenger that thrives over a wide northeastern US range. Colonies are built in underground cavities, as well as in structures, and tend to be smaller than colonies of similar species. The sturdy combs are wrapped in a fragile tan envelope, and cells in the comb are larger than those found in the combs of other species. Scavenging workers may become problematic; however, much of the behavior, and therefore the pest status, of this species is not well understood.

Southern Yellow Jacket
Vespula squamosa
Large-Colony Scavenger/Predator Yellow Jacket

L. Ames

Worker Size
½ inch (14 mm)

Colony size
500 – 4,000 workers

Colony locations
Variable, but typically subterranean. Occasionally nests in walls, and when found in natural habitats, colonies tend to be in pine forests.

Figure 2.16   Southern yellow jacket queen.

S. Marshall

Figure 2.17   Southern yellow jacket male.

The southern yellow jacket is common in Pennsylvania and southern New York, and throughout the southeastern US. Queens are predominantly orange in color, as compared to the typical yellow-and-black yellow jacket markings of workers and males. The southern yellow jacket is often known to be a social parasite of closely related species, such as the eastern and common yellow jackets. In this case a parasitic queen will take over the nest of another species, kill the existing queen, and utilize the host workers to rear her brood until all the workers are her own. Remnants of the old nest (workers and parts of the comb) are evidence of this relationship. Southern yellow jackets exist in disturbed habitats, such as yards, parks, and along roads, as well as in wooded land. They are troublesome in areas where large numbers of colonies exist in urban or suburban areas. They will scavenge for protein.

"Ground Hornet" Yellow Jacket
Vespula vidua
Small-Colony, Non-Scavenger Yellow Jacket

J. Grangloff-Kaufmann

Worker Size
¾ inch (21 mm)

Colony size
A few hundred workers. Colony duration is short compared to other yellow jackets.

Colony locations
Subterranean, under logs and in rodent burrows

Figure 2.18 A yellow jacket species commonly referred to as the "ground hornet" or the "long yellow jacket."

Although "ground hornet" yellow jacket colonies appear in disturbed areas throughout the Northeast, such as fields and yards, these wasps only present a risk to humans if the nest is disturbed. Colonies are relatively small. Members of this species will visit outdoor food areas, and will be caught in traps with food baits, but are more likely to prey upon other insects than scavenge.

Other small-colony yellow jacket species that can be found in the Northeast include *Vespula acadica* and *V. consobrina*, which are predators of live arthropods, and *V. austriaca*, which is a social parasite of closely related species. The black jacket, *V. consobrina*, has occasionally been found nesting in walls of structures. These species are not significant pests in the northeastern US, although there are reports of people being stung repeatedly after encountering colonies.

Aerial Yellow Jacket
Dolichovespula arenaria
Aerial-Nesting Yellow Jacket

Figure 2.19   Aerial yellow jacket.

Figure 2.20   Aerial yellow jackets on a new nest.

Worker Size
½ inch (14 mm)

Colony size
Up to 1,000 workers

Colony locations
Aerial paper nest

The aerial yellow jacket is a wasp that builds a volleyball-sized, gray, round paper nest with a scalloped texture on the outside. Although the size of the nest is small compared to that of the closely related bald-faced hornet, these wasps can be quite numerous and aggressive when the nest is disturbed. A colony was once found by the author in a narrow (5-inches inner diameter), hollow cavity of a log in a wooden swing set, posing a particular threat to children. Aerial yellow jackets may also build colonies high in trees, or in shrubs, attached to structures, or in other aboveground cavities. They rarely nest underground. Aerial yellow jackets are not typically scavengers for protein, but they can become a nuisance when they are attracted to sweets in late summer. They are often caught in yellow jacket traps.

A less common aerial-nesting species named *D. norvegicoides* is similar to the aerial yellow jacket but has much smaller colonies. Little is known about the biology or ecology of this species. It can be found in the northeastern US and tends to inhabit mountainous regions. A related black-and-white species, *D. arctica* is a social parasite of other aerial-nesting yellow jackets. Queens of *D. arctica* will invade an aerial-nesting yellow jacket colony early in the season, lay eggs and allow the workers to raise her own young, and will eventually kill the queen.

Bald-faced Hornet
Dolichovespula maculata
Aerial-Nesting Yellow Jacket

G. Alpert

Worker Size
⅝ – ⅞ inch (16 – 22 mm)

Colony size
Up to several hundred workers

Colony locations
Aerial paper nest

Figure 2.21   Bald-faced hornet.

W. Cranshaw, Colorado State U., Bugwood.org

UGA5024094

Figure 2.22   Bald-faced hornets guarding the colony.

Despite the name, the bald-faced hornet is not a true hornet. It is a large species of black-and-white yellow jacket, closely related to the aerial yellow jacket, *D. arenaria*. The number of colony members is smaller than other yellow jacket species, with populations of only a few hundred. The nest is usually visible as a large oval mass, wrapped in gray paper, which can reach an impressive two to three feet in length. The average size of a mature nest is in the range of 12 – 16 inches wide and 14 – 20 inches long. Nests are usually aerial, built against structures, or in the branches of trees and shrubs.

The bald-faced hornet is the only commonly occurring yellow jacket pest in the Northeast with black-and-white coloring. A similar-looking mimic species, the black jacket (*Vespula consobrina*), can be found in the northeastern US in mountainous conifer forests and is not a major pest species because it is rarely encountered. New bald-faced hornet nests are built each year, and old ones are not reused. This species can be a pest when the colony is located close to human activity. Workers will vigorously defend the colony if disturbed, but otherwise these wasps are often passive or only occasionally aggressive when encountered alone. Bald-faced hornets are not scavengers, and will search for live prey, especially caterpillars and flies caught in flight. Preying upon flies may associate bald-faced hornets with carcasses and other fly-attracting matter.

G. Alpert

Figure 2.23 Colony of bald-faced hornets on a building.

Paper Wasps

Several species—Polistes spp.

Worker Size ¾ – ⅞ inch (19 – 22 mm)
Colony size A few dozen to as many as 100 wasps
Colony locations Aerial or in structural shelters and cavities

European paper wasp
Polistes dominulus

Figure 2.24 European paper wasps on the comb.

Northern paper wasp
P. fuscatus

Figure 2.25 A Northern paper wasp.

Common paper wasps of the genus *Polistes* are often called "umbrella wasps" for the style of the nests. Each nest is made of a single-layered paper comb that is exposed, not enclosed in an envelope, although combs may be built in protected cavities. Nest locations include roof eaves; under railings, flashing, and wooden seating; in metal structures, such as fence pipes, playground equipment, undisturbed lawn equipment, and car engine compartments; as well as in shrubs. Paper wasps will also build nests sideways on vertical surfaces. They may construct colonies inside bird nesting boxes and kill hatchling birds. Paper wasps are as likely to become alarmed and sting as yellow jackets, but the number of individuals per colony is much lower. However, all members will defend the colony vigorously if disturbed. These wasps are not usually a threat when left alone, but their tendency to build nests close to human activity can make them an important pest.

Common paper wasp
P. exclamans

(CC) Larry D. Moore

Figure 2.26 A large colony of common paper wasps.

Polistes wasps forage for soft-bodied insects. It is not uncommon to see several *Polistes* workers carving up a large caterpillar to be carried back to the colony. Although their social structure is different than that of yellow jackets, *Polistes* wasps have dominant, nest-initiating females that produce broods of worker females, and reproductive males and females. Dominant females begin nests, but will sometimes take over the nests of other females. If the dominant female disappears, another female may quickly take her place. Most species of paper wasps are brown in color, but the common invasive species, *Polistes dominulus*, or the European paper wasp, resembles a yellow jacket with yellow-and-black markings. These characteristics are detailed in Figure 2.27.

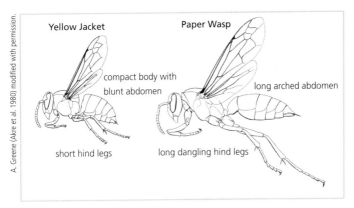

Figure 2.27   The yellow-and-black colored European paper wasp can be distinguished from a yellow jacket by comparing the shape of the gaster (abdomen), and length of the hind legs.

European Hornet
Vespa crabro

Figure 2.28 The European hornet.

Figure 2.29 European hornet nest.

Worker Size
1 – 1½ inch (26 – 38 mm)

Colony size
300 – 500 workers, sometimes more

Colony locations
Aerial, but in cavities and abandoned structures

This is the only true hornet to be found in the United States; however, it is an introduced species from Europe. The gold and brown colors of this large wasp resemble the cicada killer wasp, except that the cicada killer wasp is distinctly larger with white spots, and is ground-nesting and solitary. European hornets are much more likely to sting than cicada killer wasps, but they are less common in urban areas, and prefer rural farmland, orchards, and old barns. Occasionally, they do appear in urban areas when habitat is available. Colonies are usually built in hollow trees and abandoned wooden structures. Nests resemble those of bald-faced hornets but are usually tan in color and never hang freely from branches.

European hornets are aggressive when defending the nest, but calm while foraging for their diet of insects and ripe fruits. Workers will hunt at night and sometimes bang against lighted windows. They can damage saplings and tender branches of ornamental woody plants as they strip the bark and girdle stems to collect sap, and also use bark fibers for nest building. Workers may also girdle and kill whole plants.

M. Malinoski

Figure 2.30　Damage to a woody plant from European hornets.

Social and Solitary Bees (Moderate Risk)

Bees are closely related to wasps but differ in some important biological and ecological ways. Bees thrive on pollen and nectar, rather than preying on insects or scavenging, and therefore serve a crucial role as pollinators. Bees have longer and denser branched hairs on their bodies and appear fuzzy, a feature that helps in pollen collection. Social bees that build combs utilize wax produced by their bodies rather than wood fiber for the comb structure.

Bees readily defend their colonies but are not usually as aggressive as wasps. Honey bees are vigorous defenders of the colony as they guard their stores of honey, pollen, and larvae from other animals. Social bumble bees build small colonies in structural and soil cavities and tend to be docile while foraging. However, when disturbed, a colony of bumble bees may swarm an intruder and sting repeatedly. Solitary bees, such as carpenter and ground-nesting bees, do not live in colonies, do not build large nests, and rear only a few young. Measurable economic risks are associated with some bees. Carpenter bees can inflict damage to structural wood of houses, decks, and other objects, while ground-nesting bees can deter golfers or athletes from playing their sport in infested areas.

European Honey Bee
Apis mellifera mellifera

Figure 2.31 The European honey bee.

Figure 2.32 The wax comb of a honey bee hive.

Worker Size
½ inch (14 mm)

Colony size
Up to 20,000 – 60,000 workers and up to several hundred drones

Colony locations
Natural and man-made cavities

Honey bees are man's most valuable insect. Honey bees are the most important pollinators of nearly one-third of all food crops, and when managed in colonies, they are considered livestock. They must be protected whenever possible. Honey bees, imported to the Americas from Europe and other countries beginning in the 1600s, are yellow-orange, orange-brown, or even black, usually with striped abdomens, and have a fuzzy appearance. They build large perennial nests that survive for several years. Colonies that are established in structural cavities can create a potential risk to humans if they are disturbed.

Honey bees commonly swarm when the colony becomes too big for their living space or when new queens are produced. A swarm will appear as a cloud of bees or, when resting, as a large mass in a tree or shrub, or on a man-made object. When

continued on p.65...

Africanized Honey Bee – *Apis mellifera scutellata*

Dr. Nicholas W. Calderone, Cornell University

Africanized honey bees are the result of the importation of African honey bees to Brazil in the 1950s for the purpose of breeding a stock of bees that was adapted to tropical conditions. The African bees escaped into the wild where they began reproducing and mating with European bees, thereby producing the Africanized, or "killer" bees. The Africanized bee rapidly colonized most of South and Central America. They were first detected in the US in 1990 in Hidalgo, Texas. As of 2006, they have colonized much of the southwestern US, including most of Texas, southern New Mexico, Arizona, southern Nevada, and the southern third of California. They have also become established in central Florida. **They are not known to be in any part of the northeastern United States at this time.**

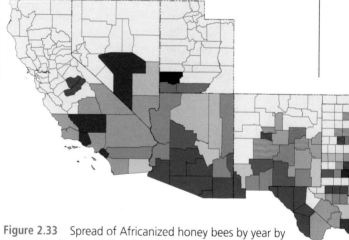

Figure 2.33 Spread of Africanized honey bees by year by county. Updated July 2009. First found in southern Texas in 1990, Africanized honey bees are now found in much of the South.

Africanized honey bees are nearly indistinguishable from their European counterparts. There are no genetic tests available to assess the degree of Africanization; however, there are subtle differences in a number of physical traits, including wing length, and morphometric (physical trait) analysis can be used to determine the degree of Africanization. If you think that a colony may be Africanized, contact your state Department of Agriculture.

Behaviorally, Africanized bees are noticeably different from European bees. Most conspicuous is their greater level of defensive behavior. Africanized bees are more easily disturbed and quicker to sting, respond in greater numbers, and will follow a fleeing victim a greater distance. However, individual bees can only sting once, and their venom is no more toxic than that found in European bees. As with most stinging insects, bees are only defensive around their nest. Bees in the landscape pose no threat, except that they may sting if stepped upon. Africanized bees also swarm more often than their European relatives, and their choice of nest site locations varies more widely.

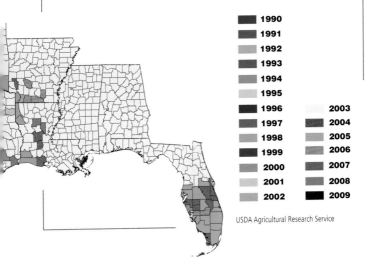

■ 1990	
■ 1991	
▨ 1992	
■ 1993	
■ 1994	
▨ 1995	
■ 1996	▨ 2003
■ 1997	■ 2004
▨ 1998	▨ 2005
■ 1999	▨ 2006
▨ 2000	■ 2007
▨ 2001	▨ 2008
▨ 2002	■ 2009

USDA Agricultural Research Service

S. Bauer, USDA Agricultural Research Service

Figure 2.34 Working with Africanized bees.

The limit to the natural spread of Africanized bees is unknown, although the long winters and cold temperatures of the interior portions of the United States may prove inhospitable. Colonization will probably occur throughout the southern states and along the coasts as far north as northern California and North Carolina. This includes major wintering grounds for migratory beekeepers and the majority of production areas for queen and package bees that are purchased each year by beekeepers. The annual migration of bees for pollination from southern wintering locations to orchards and fields in the North and West may facilitate the spread of Africanized bees. Even in places where Africanized bees are present in high numbers, their presence has not caused major problems in the US.

...continued from p.61

swarming, honey bees are of little risk, but it is inadvisable for anyone to use loud or vibrating equipment, such as a lawn-mower, nearby until the swarm has gone away. Honey bees can be very defensive when the colony is threatened but can also be handled easily by a skilled beekeeper. Workers will sting, but each worker can only sting one time. The stinger is barbed, which forces the bee to rip its venom sac and stinger from the abdomen, resulting in its death. The stinger remains embed-ded, and the attached gland continues to pump venom into the victim. When away from the hive, honey bees are quite docile. It has been reported that on cool, cloudy days, honey bee colonies tend to be "irritable," or easily aroused, while on sunny, warm days, they are usually calmer.

R. Blohm

Figure 2.35 A honey bee swarm.

While honey bees suffer from several parasitic mites and diseases that affect the brood, there are second-ary pests associated with old honey bee colonies that can become structural pests in buildings. These include wax moths, dermestid bee-tles, and many species of ants that may feed on left-over honey. The develop-ment of mold may also be-come an issue. In late 2006, beekeepers in the United States began noticing the abrupt disappearance of adult worker bees from colonies. The phenomenon became known as Colony Collapse Disorder, and this has devastated bee colonies in many parts of the US and other countries. No clear cause has been determined as of the writing of this guide.

Bumble Bees
Bombus species

Figure 2.36A Bumble bee (Bombus spp.) on flower.

Figure 2.36B Bumble bee (Bombus spp.) on flower.

Worker Size
Variable, up to about 1 inch (26 mm)

Colony size
50 – 400

Colony locations
Subterranean or occasionally structural cavities

There are about 50 species of bumble bees in the United States. Bumble bees are robust, social insects with bodies densely covered in branched hairs, and vividly colored in black and yellow or orange. They build medium-sized colonies of several hundred workers that occasionally become a problem in areas of human activity. Queens are the only colony members to survive winter. In early spring the queen will seek a cavity such as an abandoned rodent burrow, old bird nest, hay bale, or an occasional structural cavity close to the ground. Queen bees raise the first brood on a ball of honey and pollen until workers emerge to take over colony duties. Bumble bees are fairly docile and unlikely to sting when foraging, but will vigorously defend the colony if it is disturbed. They can sting repeatedly, like wasps. Generally, immediate control is not recommended, since bumble bees are very important native pollinators. However, prevention of nest building in the same location the following year is suggested. If the colony is located in or close to an occupied structure and bees present a threat to humans, control may be warranted.

Eric Gamble, flickr.com

Figure 2.37 A bumble bee nest with larvae.

Carpenter Bee
Xylocopa virginica

Figure 2.38 A carpenter bee female.

Figure 2.39 Carpenter bee galleries in structural wood.

Worker Size
¾ – 1 inch (21 – 26 mm)

Colony size
Solitary, but several may occupy the same area

Colony locations
Sound wood, fascia boards, exposed heartwood of trees, structural wood

Carpenter bees are often mistaken for large bumble bees, but they are different in many ways. The most common pest species in the Northeast, the eastern carpenter bee (*Xylocopa virginica*) has yellow hair with a shiny black bald spot on the thorax, and a black, mostly hairless abdomen. Unlike bumble bees, carpenter bees are solitary insects that bore tunnels into the wood of trees or structures to create long galleries for egg laying and raising brood. They can inflict damage to a wood structure through years of excavating tunnels. Wood may become weakened and susceptible to fungal rot. Although carpenter bees may appear aggressive, most people encounter the males defending territory and females. Males cannot sting and pose little threat to humans, but they will hover and guard their territory against intruding males. The male will often fly boldly toward people in a seemingly aggressive manner. However, these bees use objects, including people, as landmarks to maintain territories. Females have stingers but never seek to sting, and will do so only if handled roughly. Although they are solitary, several males and females may occupy the same area, giving the appearance of a colony. Risk is considered "moderate" due to the type of damage that can be inflicted on structural and decorative wood and the challenge of managing carpenter bees on a long-term basis.

Solitary Wasps and Bees (Low or No Risk)

Solitary wasps and bees rear only a few young in burrows or galleries that are dug in soil or wood, or built on objects in their environment. They do not exhibit defensive behaviors on the scale of their social cousins because they do not guard large caches of resources (food or larvae). Solitary bees are vital pollinators, and most solitary wasps are predators of other insects. All are beneficial in the environment and should be conserved, wherever possible.

Mud Daubers, Potter Wasps, and Mason Wasps
Eumeninae, Sphecidae

Figure 2.40   A mason wasp.

Worker Size
⅜ – 1 inch (10 – 25 mm)

Colony size
Solitary, but several may occupy the same area

Colony locations
Various sizes and shapes of mud nests on buildings, fences, plants, rocks, and occasionally in small cavities

Figure 2.41   The mud nest of a potter wasp.

Mud daubers are medium to large wasps with very narrow and long waists (petioles), which earn them the name "thread-waisted" wasps. They have long, thin legs wings, and antennae. Some are dark-colored with metallic tones of blue and violet, and others are yellow and brown or black. Characteristic behavior includes flitting their wings and quick, erratic, and jerky movements. Mud daubers construct nests of mud for rearing young. Masses of cylindrical mud tubes (resembling organ pipes) are built on the sides of structures. Females provision each nest chamber with one egg and several spiders or insect larvae. The new wasps emerge the following spring. One common species, the blue mud dauber, does not make a nest of its own. The female relies on similar species of wasps to build

Figure 2.42 Nest of the organ pipe mud dauber.

Figure 2.43 The blue mud wasp.

mud tubes. She will then remove the contents and replace them with her own eggs and prey. Mud daubers can sting if handled, but are not aggressive or inclined to sting. They do not linger near the nest to defend it.

Potter wasps are beneficial predators that create underground or exposed mud nests of various styles where eggs are laid and provisioned with insects and spiders. Potter wasps may also use existing cavities, such as man-made holes or tunnels created by other insects. The developing larva will overwinter in the nest and emerge in the spring as an adult. These wasps are delicate with long legs, wings, and a long, thin petiole. Different species will vary in color and may appear dark colored with white, yellow, orange, or red stripes, similar to more dangerous wasps, such as yellow jackets. They are effective predators and not a threat to human health.

Another group, called digger wasps, provisions larvae in burrows with insects and spiders. They may reuse old burrows or dig new ones, but they do not create mud structures for egg laying.

If mud nests are considered unsightly, they can be physically removed from the structure with a scraping tool or a strong jet of water. However, toleration and conservation of these wasps is encouraged because they are beneficial predators and pollinators.

W. Cranshaw, Colorado State U., Bugwood.org

Figure 2.44 A digger wasp with her prey.

Eastern Cicada Killer Wasp
Sphecius speciosus

S.B. Jacobs

Figure 2.45 The Eastern cicada killer wasp.

Worker Size
1 – 1½ inches (26 – 40 mm)

Colony size
Solitary, but many wasps may occupy the same area

Colony locations
Subterranean

K.R. Law, USDA APHIS PPQ, Bugwood.org

Figure 2.46 An Eastern cicada killer wasp burrow entrance with cicadas.

Cicada killer wasps are among the largest wasps found in the northeastern US; they belong to the family *Crabrionidae*. The eastern cicada killer wasp is brown with black-and-yellow markings on the abdomen, and amber wings. Females dig burrows for egg laying and provision their young with cicadas that have been captured and paralyzed with a sting. The stinger of a female wasp is blunt and is not used primarily for defense. Cicada killer wasps, although solitary, may appear in large numbers in favorable nesting spots, such as sandy or well-drained soils in sunny locations, home lawns, flower beds, school and park grounds, and frequently in golf course sand traps. Perception of such large wasps is often negative and fearful due to these insects' energetic flight activity and perhaps the distinct buzz of their wings. Males vigorously guard their territory from other males; but like other solitary wasps and bees, male cicada killer wasps cause concern without having the ability to sting. They will investigate new objects, including humans, in their territory behavior that mimics defense. Cicada killer wasps can create mounds of soil in turf areas or excavate soil from between stones in stone walls, spoiling their appearance. However, these wasps provide natural control of cicadas and other arthropods, and may be beneficial to the trees damaged by cicada egg laying. They are active for a relatively short period of time, about 60 to 75 days, from July to late September, and they should be tolerated if possible.

Other closely related and commonly encountered wasps in the family Crabrionidae are known as sand wasps, genus *Bembix*. They are stout-bodied, beneficial, and harmless wasps that dig burrows in the soil and provision larvae with a stockpile of spiders and other soft-bodied prey. There may be numerous wasps in a small area giving the impression of a swarm. Again, these nonaggressive wasps are active for a short period during the year, and they should be tolerated if possible.

Scoliid Wasps
Scoliidae

Figure 2.47   The blue-winged wasp.

Worker Size
¾ inch (20 mm)

Colony size
No colony; solitary females lay eggs on beetle grubs in grassy areas. Several may occupy the same area

Colony locations
Athletic fields and lawns

Scoliid wasps are a small family of beneficial parasitic wasps. One of the most common of the Scoliid wasps is the blue-winged wasp, *Scolia dubia*. Though not commonly considered a pest, they can cause problems in the landscape when they do appear. This species is a robust, dark-colored wasp with cream or yellow spots on the sides of the abdomen, fine golden hairs, and bluish metallic wings. Blue-winged wasps are attracted to turfgrass infested with May/June beetle larvae (*Scarabidae*). They can be seen flying close to the ground on athletic fields in midsummer. Blue-winged wasp females dig in the soil to find beetle grubs, then paralyze and lay an egg on each grub. Blue-winged wasps are beneficial predators of some turfgrass grubs and not aggressive, nor do they sting. However, they may be distracting and upsetting to people who encounter them. The key to managing blue-winged wasps is to reduce May and June beetle grub populations in valued turfgrass fields, using the principles of IPM.

Spider Wasps
Pompilidae

S. Ellis, USDA, Bugwood.org

Figure 2.48   A spider wasp with prey.

Worker Size
Various, but commonly less than 1 inch (25mm)

Colony size
Solitary, individual brood chambers

Colony locations
Subterranean burrows

Spider wasps are solitary hunters of spiders. Females capture and paralyze spiders, drag them to burrows dug in the soil, and lay a single egg on each. Wasp larvae feed on the paralyzed spiders, grow, and eventually spin silken cocoons for pupation. Most offspring emerge the following year. Spider wasps are fairly conspicuous insects, with coloration ranging from orange and black, to black with a metallic blue sheen. They are long-legged wasps that dart rapidly along the ground and flit their wings. Common species are large enough to elicit fear in the onlooker, though these wasps are docile and unlikely to sting. They should be tolerated as much as possible.

Ground-Nesting Bees

Many species

Worker Size
⅛ – ¾ inch (4 – 20 mm)

Colony size
Solitary, but communal (many will occupy the same area)

Colony locations
Subterranean

Figure 2.49   A ground-nesting or plasterer bee in her burrow. (Close-up above.)

Many species of solitary ground-nesting bees can be found in sunny, dry, and sandy areas of parks, golf courses, and other open spaces. They may also occupy shadier sites with loose, well-drained soil with little vegetation. Plasterer bees are one type commonly seen in urban-suburban landscapes and are sometimes considered pests. These bees tend to aggregate nests as though they are part of a large colony; however, they actually create individual burrows in the soil and tolerate their neighbors. Occasionally females will share burrows but dig individual tunnels from a single entrance. Males, which do not sting, are most frequently encountered as they defend territory in hopes of mating with females that are burrowing and laying eggs. These bees can become quite numerous and troublesome in areas frequented by humans, such as parks, golf courses, and home lawns. Problems lie in people's perception of the risk of being stung. If they are not a serious nuisance, any species of ground-nesting bees should be left alone. Their value as pollinators is underestimated, and control can be challenging. The window of adult activity is typically only a few weeks long, after which time they disappear. Mulch and ground cover, including thicker turfgrass, discourage these bees from nesting in home lawn and garden areas.

Giant Resin Bee
Megachile sculpturalis

Figure 2.50   A giant resin bee.

Worker Size
½ – almost 1 inch (14 – 24 mm)

Colony size
Solitary, but females nest close together

Colony locations
Existing holes in wooden structures

The giant resin bee is an introduced species from Asia that has become established in the southeastern United States and expanded through the northeastern US and into Canada. It is a highly visible species because of its robust size and tendency to nest around structures in carpenter bee nest holes, as well as between boards of decks and siding. Males will hover and guard nest sites in the same way as do carpenter bee males. Their coloring is black and dark yellow, although the abdomen is dull, not shiny black, as are carpenter bees' abdomens. Despite having large mandibles (jaws), giant resin bees do not inflict damage on structural wood, and they are unlikely to sting, making the species basically harmless. They are often confused with carpenter bees, due to size, coloration, and use of the same nest sites. Giant resin bees feed on pollen and nectar as do other bees.

Appendix: Quick identification of wasps and bees and sting risk level

Type	Physical description	Nest type and location	Risk level
Yellow jacket *Vespula* species	Yellow and black bands, ½ – ¾ inch; few hairs, blunt abdomen at waist	Multilevel paper combs with envelope; structures and ground cavities.	High
Aerial yellow jacket *Dolichovespula arenaria*	Yellow and black bands, ½ inch; few hairs, blunt abdomen at waist	Multilevel paper combs in small, delicate, ball-shaped gray scalloped envelope; in aboveground cavities and on structures, shrubs, and trees.	High
Bald-faced hornet *Dolichovespula maculata*	White and black bands, ⅝ – ⅞ inch, nearly hairless	Multilevel paper combs in large, ball-shaped gray envelope; in shrubs and trees.	High
Paper or umbrella wasp *Polistes* species	Yellow, black bands or gold to brown/black; hairless, rounded abdomen at waist, long dangling legs, ¾ – ⅞ inch	Umbrella paper nest with visible comb; often under eaves or in protected spots, including shrubs.	High

Appendix: Quick identification of wasps and bees and sting risk level
(continued)

Type	Physical description	Nest type and location	Risk level
European hornet *Vespa crabro*	Gold and brown/black, some hairs, 1 – 1½ inches	Multilevel paper combs in ovoid-shaped, red-brown envelope; in abandoned structures or hollow trees.	High if colony is disturbed
Honey bee *Apis mellifera*	Gold, orange, and brown, fuzzy or hairy, ½ inch	Large social colonies in natural or man-made cavities.	Medium
Bumble bee *Bombus* species	Yellow to orange and black or all black, fuzzy or hairy; up to 1 inch	Small social colonies in natural or man-made cavities.	Medium
Cicada killer wasp *Sphecius speciosus*	Large (almost 2 inches); black and yellow with brown stripes; female larger than male	Solitary; males guard nest holes, females dig holes in sandy or well-drained soils with little ground cover, sunny locations.	Low, but perceived to be dangerous
Ground-nesting bee Many species	Variable black and yellow to orange or metallic, usually with hairy bodies; various sizes from ⅛ to ¾ inch	Solitary, but found in groups; nests are holes in sandy or well-drained soils with little ground cover, sunny locations.	Low, but perceived to be dangerous

Type	Physical description	Nest type and location	Risk level
Carpenter bee *Xylocopa* species	Large, black with some yellow hairs on thorax, black abdomen; ¾ – 1 inch	Solitary; males guard nest holes; females gnaw round holes and long galleries in exposed wood.	Low
Mud daubers, mason wasps, and potter wasps Eumeninae, Sphecidae	Thin, delicate, various colors, including metallic blue-violet and brown/gold ⅜ to 1 inch	Solitary; nests constructed of mud into tubes, pots, or mounds on vertical surfaces, stone and brick buildings.	Low
Blue-winged wasp (Scoliid Wasp) *Scolia dubia*	Large (¾ to over 1 inch) black wasps with 6 or so yellow spots on abdomen	Solitary; females fly low over turf looking for grubs, on which they lay eggs.	Low
Spider wasp Pompilidae	Thin, leggy, spider-like and black with metallic blue-violet sheen, curly antennae; less than 1 inch	Solitary; underground nest cells in well-drained, sandy soils.	Low
Giant resin bee *Megachile sculpturalis*	Stout black bee with yellow hairs, body ½ to 1 inch long, Blunt abdomen, wings dark but transparent	Solitary; females use existing tubes and holes, sealed with resin from sap	Low

References

Akre, R.D., A. Greene, J.F. MacDonald, P.J. Landolt, and H.G. Davis. 1981. *Yellowjackets of America North of Mexico*. U.S. Department of Agriculture Handbook 552.

Aldrich, J.R., J.P. Kochansky, J.D. Sexton. 1985. Chemical attraction of the eastern yellowjacket, *Vespula maculifrons* (Hymenoptera: Vespidae). *Cellular and Molecular Life Sciences*, Vol. 41, No. 3, 420-422.

Braband, L., J. Gangloff-Kaufmann, C. Klass, J. Rodler. Stinging Insect IPM Research, Demonstration and Outreach Project, NYS IPM Program, 2004. Online at: HTTP://NYSIPM. CORNELL.EDU.

Delaplane, K.S. 2006. *Africanized Honey Bees*. University of Georgia Cooperative Extension, Bulletin 1290. Online at: HTTP://WWW.ENT.UGA.EDU.

Goddard, J. 2003. *Physician's Guide to Arthropods of Medical Importance* (4th Ed.). CRC Press, LLC., New York, NY.

Gold, R.E. and S.C. Jones. 2000. *Handbook of Household and Structural Insect Pests*. Entomological Society of America. Lanham, MD.

Hood, W.M. 1999. *Honey Bee Colony Removal from Structures*. Clemson University HGIC Publication No. 2507. Online at: HTTP://HGIC.CLEMSON.EDU.

Kondo, T., M.L. Williams, R. Minckley. 2000. Giant Resin Bees! Exotic Bee Species Makes Its Way from East Coast to Alabama. *Highlights of Agricultural Research*, Vol. 47, No 3. Alabama Agricultural Experiment Station.

Mallis, A. 2004. *Handbook of Pest Control*. 9th edition. GIE Media, Inc.

Mussen, E.C. UC Pest Notes: Bee and Wasp Stings. University of California Statewide IPM Program, ANR Publication 7449. Online at: HTTP://WWW.IPM.UCDAVIS.EDU.

Pinto, L. J. and S.K. Kraft. 2000. Action Thresholds in School IPM Programs: Supplemental Materials for IPM Training Manual. Maryland Department of Agriculture.

Ross, K.G. and R.W. Matthews. 1991. *The Social Biology of Wasps*. Comstock Publishing Associates, Ithaca, NY.

Smith, E.H. and R.C. Whitman. 1992. *NPCA Field Guide to Structural Pests*. National Pest Control Association. Dunn Loring, VA.

Visscher, P.K., R.S. Vetter, and S. Camazine. 1996. Removing bee stings. *Lancet*, 348: 301-302.

Wegener, G.S. and K. Jordan. 2005. Comparison of three liquid lures for trapping social wasps (Hymenoptera: Vespidae). *J. Econ. Entomology*, 98(3): 664-666.

Additional Resources

Further Reading

Aebi, O. and H. Aebi. *Mastering the Art of Beekeeping*. Unity Press, Santa Cruz, CA. 1979.

Buchmann, S. L., and G. P. Nabhan. *The Forgotten Pollinators*. Island Press, Washington, D.C. 1997.

Graham, J.M. *The Hive and the Honeybee*. Dadant and Sons, Hamilton, IL. 1992.

Heinrich, B. *Bumblebee Economics*. Harvard University Press, Cambridge, MA. 1979.

Kearns, C., and J. Thomson. *The Natural History of Bumblebees. A Sourcebook for Investigations*. University Press of Colorado, Boulder, CO. 2001.

Mader, E., M. Spivak, and E. Evans. *Managing Alternative Pollinators: A Handbook for Beekeepers, Growers, and Conservationists*, NRAES-186. Natural Resource, Agriculture, and Engineering Service, Ithaca, NY. 2010.

O'Toole, C., and A. Raw. *Bees of the World*. Blandford, London, U.K. 1999.

Procter, M., P. Yeo, and A. Lack. *The Natural History of Pollination*. Timber Press, Portland, OR. 1996.

von Frisch, K. *The Dancing Bees*. Harcourt Brace and Co. New York, NY. 1955.

Winston, M.L. *The Biology of the Honey Bee*. Harvard University Press, Cambridge, MA. 1987.

Xerces Society for Invertebrate Conservation at HTTP://WWW.XERCES.ORG or at: 4828 SE Hawthorne Blvd. Portland, Oregon 97215 (503-232-6639). Information and resources about bumble bee and other pollinator conservation.

Control of turfgrass insects for indirect control of predatory wasps

Brandenburg, R.L. and M.G. Villani. *Handbook of Turfgrass Insect Pests*. The Entomological Society of America. Lanham, MD. 1995.

Vittum, P.J., M.G. Villani, H. Tashiro. *Turfgrass Insects of the United States and Canada*. Comstock Publishing Associates, Ithaca, NY. 1999.

Insect images

The independent database of insect images WWW.BUGGUIDE.NET.

The University of Georgia's Bugwood site at WWW.INSECTIMAGES.ORG.

Equipment and Supplies

American Beekeeping Federation at HTTP://WWW.ABFNET.ORG, or at P.O. Box 1337, Jesup, GA 31598-1038 (mailing) or 115 Morning Glory Circle, Jesup, GA 31546 (street),

Phone (912) 427-4233. A list of resources is maintained here for beekeeping equipment and supplies, plus research news.

BeeSource at HTTP://WWW.BEESOURCE.COM. An online sourcebook for beekeeping.

BioQuip Products, Inc. at HTTP://WWW.BIOQUIP.COM, or 2321 Gladwick Street, Rancho Dominguez, CA 90220, Phone: (310) 667-8800. Suppliers of various entomological equipment and educational materials; bee suits and other protective equipment; insect collecting supplies.

Wildlife Control Supplies, WWW.WILDLIFECONTROLSUPPLIES.COM. They offer weep hole covers, personal protective gear for dealing with stinging insects, and tools.